Welcome to the world of
POCKETTES

This new, easy-to-carry, take-along reading is designed for people on the go!

POCKETTES, produced by Pocket Books for today's fast-paced society, is a collection of exciting mysteries, stirring romances and thrilling gothic adventures—all specially selected to provide a satisfying and pleasurable reading experience that can be enjoyed and completed in an afternoon or evening.

Authored by world-famous, best-selling writers such as Faith Baldwin, Gertrude Schweitzer, Benjamin Siegel, Adela Rogers St. Johns, Jerome Weidman, Dorothy Eden, Vera Caspary, Frank Yerby, and many, many more, **POCKETTES** will indeed bring you "the finest in reading at the lowest possible price."

If you wish to purchase other **POCKETTE** titles and cannot find them at your local bookstore, please use the convenient order coupon at the back of this book.

MORE...

POCKETTES
for people on the go

50¢ each

NO. OF COPIES	BOOK NO.	TITLE AND AUTHOR
....	50601	THE DOCTOR, Benjamin Siegel
....	50602	RUTH, Vera Caspary
....	50603	THE HOUSE BY THE SEA, Mignon Eberhart
....	50604	MISS ELIZABETH LANDON, M.D., Gertrude Schweitzer
....	50605	A LINNET SINGING, Dorothy Eden
....	50607	THE DANGEROUS MRS. MALONE, Adela Rogers St. Johns
....	50608	"I, AND I ALONE", Jerome Weidman
....	50609	MAGDA, Faith Baldwin

POCKETTES, Dept. F-1
Simon & Schuster, Inc., 1 West 39th St.
New York, N.Y. 10018

Send me titles checked above. I enclose .50 per copy plus .25 for postage and handling.

Name...

Address...

City...

State...Zip...................................

In **A Linnet Singing,** Dorothy Eden, one of the world's greatest authors, has written a love story of unusual beauty and poignancy.

Each year, Finch saved his money. Soon he would have enough to take the trip he had always dreamed of. He and his beautiful birds would leave the harsh, cold world of Victorian England forever.

A warm land beckoned—a land of sunshine and flowers. He already had his reservation.

Then he met Gilly. Gilly, who needed him.

His dream would have to wait until she got better. There was no beauty anywhere without her.

A LINNET
SINGING

Dorothy Eden

POCKETTES
Published by POCKET BOOKS

A LINNET SINGING

Pockette edition published March, 1972

 _____

This Pockette edition is printed from brand-new plates made
from completely reset, clear, easy-to-read type. Pockette
editions are published by POCKET BOOKS, a division of
Simon & Schuster, Inc., 630 Fifth Avenue, New York,
N. Y. 10020. Trademarks registered in the United States
and other countries.

L

Finch had to be up long before daylight to feed his birds, tidy his room and get to the office two miles away on foot across London Bridge and down the narrow muddy thoroughfares, jostling with hackney cabs, drays, barrow boys and pedestrians, to Lincolns Inn Fields by eight o'clock.

If he were five minutes late Mr. Trumper had the greatest pleasure in rapping his knuckles with the heavy round ruler whose proper use was for drawing meticulous red lines down the sides of deed paper. Mr. Trumper found Finch's reddened bony knuckles much more interesting than deed paper. He frequently predicted that

Finch would not in a hundred years make a law clerk. The wonder was that Mr. Sampson retained his services. Idle, lazy young varmint. Always dreaming about catching and keeping linnets and larks and such. Childish nonsense. A hard-working ambitious young man couldn't afford time for such a hobby, or indeed for any hobby. He worked twelve hours a day six days of the week and on Sundays properly went to church and said his thanks to the Almighty. And in due course, if he was industrious, the Almighty made him a law clerk, like Mr. Trumper, with ink-stained fingers, a long pinched nose, and a ruler in his hand.

What Mr. Trumper didn't know was that Finch had no intention whatever of becoming a law clerk. He had much bigger dreams which didn't include a high stool in a legal office, and endless deeds full of wherefores and herein-afters. In a way the office, to him, was like the cages to his birds. The birds twittered constant-ly and hopefully about light and freedom, and so did Finch. If he seemed to Mr. Trumper to remain irritatingly cheerful in spite of looking constantly half-starved and hollow-cheeked, it was because already he had almost enough saved out of his meagre salary to realise his dream. Within three months he would have sufficient. He had already written to a shipping company about buying a passage to the distant colony, New Zealand, as far off as a star, on one of their high-masted sailing ships.

"We'll soon be on our way," he told his birds as he put their cages in the lightest spot his basement room offered. This was at the window which, when the daylight grew stronger, afforded a view of the swishing skirts of women held delicately out of the mud and occasionally displaying a tantalising glimpse of a slender ankle, and the trousered and gaitered legs of men.

"There'll be blue skies and sun out there," he went on. "No more dark rooms or dusty offices for you nor me. We're going to stretch our wings. Come along, my beauties. Hey, what's this blocking the window?"

It looked like a bundle of old clothes. But Finch knew that if it were old clothes someone, in this poor area, would have scooped it up as treasure hours ago. Unless it had been left there only recently.

He hoped it hadn't been there long, for the weather was bitterly cold. And he was all too familiar with what an apparent bundle of rags lying in an alley or pressed up against a wall, could be. Some poor soul, drunk or starving, who had died in the night.

"Not right against my window!" he muttered, his long plain face wrinkled in distress and distaste. He was young and still not callous about suffering. He would have to succour this poor wretch if he were not too late. The night had been freezing, with a drenching white mist, and the foghorns sounding from the river like melancholy bitterns.

He expected a pallid wrinkled bearded face to look up from the rags as he gently turned the body over.

Not the white face of a girl with little more than a child's face.

Her bare feet were tucked beneath her draggled skirts. A smear of hair, yellow-y coloured, stuck to her cheek. Her hands were knotted into fists, as if in defiance against her misery.

Finch thought she was dead. But as he tried to open the poor little frozen fists she stirred. Her eyes opened and her face twisted with fear. She tried to shrink away from him, as if she would sink through the ground and be done with it all.

She'd been persecuted, thought Finch grimly. And starved. She was as light in his arms as one of his birds.

"Leave me!" she managed to whisper.

"You're frozen," he said. "Come on in. I've got no more than porridge but I'll hot it up."

The birds set up a twitter as he came in with his burden. Their noise made the drooping head on his arm move again, panic in its weakness. She was as scared as a trapped bird, and no more, he thought, than eleven years old. He didn't want to ask her what had happened to her. It would only make his fury and helplessness about all the irremediable wrongs of the poor rise choking in him again. It was the thing he was meaning to escape from. God never meant people to live like this. He had put the sun in the sky for them.

He thought instead, with a rueful grin, that old Trumper was going to be mad at him this morning, for he'd be late, as sure as fate. And he doubted old Trumper, with his long nose perpetually pinching over the spidery writing of the law, would think keeping a starving child alive more important than punctuality.

"It's only my birds making that noise," he said. "Don't let it scare you."

He laid her, rags and all, on his bed and drew the blanket over her, grinning down, not blaming her when she seemed terrified by his ugly mug. He saw now that she was older than he had first thought, probably about fifteen, for there were the smallest buds of breasts beneath her bodice. His hand had inadvertently touched one and its softness had startled him. But apart from that sign of feminity there wasn't much about her to make his blood stir. She was no oil-painting, dirt-streaked, skinny, her eyes starting out of her head. He'd like to have washed her face there and then. But it seemed more important to get the hot porridge into her before she snuffed out from fright, as well as from cold and hunger.

She could only manage three spoonfuls. By that time she was asleep, her head on his shoulder. He lay her down gently and wished he had another blanket to put over her. All he could do was cover her with his deplorably shabby overcoat. If he walked briskly he could do very well without it himself. He pondered and decided there was nothing else he could do for her except leave the plate of porridge on the table so that she could finish it when she woke.

He thought again, frowning. Compared with her, he was rich. He would leave her half a crown. By going hungry for a week or so he would have it replaced in the tin under the loose floorboard. It wouldn't mean he couldn't buy his ticket from the shipping company at the end of February.

Probably this poor little scrap had never seen

a half crown in her life. It would make her open her eyes wide when she woke up. He would like to be there to see her.

On an impulse he got his quill pen and bottle of ink and writing paper out of the cupboard and wrote in large legible writing.

I have to go to work now or I will lose my job. Finish the porridge when you wake up and talk a bit to my birds before you go. This money will buy you a bed for a few nights. If you was to spend a few pence on a decent gown you'd more likely get yourself a job. Good luck.

It only occurred to him when he was half way to the Strand that she probably couldn't read.

Well, anyway, she'd know what money was. She'd have flown when he got back this evening, and, for all her youth and innocence, he hoped it wouldn't be to squander his hard-saved money on gin.

Mr. Trumper's thick black brows had never looked so menacing.

"Well, Mr. Stevenson, what have you to say for yourself?"

"I'm late, sir."

"You call twenty-one minutes late! I call it absymally late. Absymally! I hope you have a good reason."

"Well, sir—" No use to tell Mr. Trumper, with his heart a lump of tallow fat like the candles he lit with such miserliness, about the girl. He would have said it was a case for the authorities. Leave her where she lay and let the authorities do their duty. "One of my birds was

15

sick," he said, and knew this as well was the wrong thing to say.

"Sometimes, Mr. Stevenson," Mr. Trumper ejaculated, with his scorching sarcasm, "I'm convinced you were given a bird brain yourself. Before long we shall have twitterings and whistlings in the office, no doubt. Very pretty. Very cheerful." One of the other clerks began to snicker and Mr. Trumper rapped his ruler on the desk. "This is the last time I shall be lenient, Mr. Stevenson. If you are so much as a minute late between now and next Christmas you go. Seek other employment. Yes, sir. And you can thank me for giving you one last chance. Now get to work. I shall expect you to stay an hour late tonight to recompense. Do you understand?"

"Yes, sir."

"I should hope so. A sick bird, indeed! Spending all your wages on bird-seed. It's unnatural. Frankly, Mr. Stevenson, it's my personal opinion that you're daft."

Daft to dream of blue skies, fresh air, and as much green country as the eye could see? Daft

16

to want to escape from the wretched streets where children lie down and freeze to death?

Some day, Finch thought, he would write a letter to Mr. Trumper.

"Do you remember," he would write, "when you told me I had a bird brain? I expect you are still sitting on that stool ruining your eyes in bad light, taking into your lungs all that yellow fog, while I am basking in sunshine, listening to the birds singing, planting my own piece of ground, being *free!*"

The vision, Finch found, impossible to put into words. His heart was swelling again with the excitement and optimism. In just three months he'd be going aboard the *Flying Scud.* . . .

He had quite forgotten the waif in his room, and indeed didn't give her another thought until he was ready to go home that evening. Then he reflected with some regret on his vanished half crown. For it would be vanished, that he could swear.

At first he thought weariness and light-headedness (he had gone without lunch to save a penny towards the lost half crown) were making him imagine things, such as the coin untouched on the table and a small unobtrusive shape still in his bed.

He hastily struck a match and lit the lamp. His birds stirred and twittered faintly. The shape in the bed didn't move.

She was dead! She had died most inconveniently in his bed!

He shook her, not too gently, and was disproportionately relieved when he found her body limp and warm. No rigor mortis yet. Not in his bed, He'd have found that hard to explain not only to his landlady, Mrs. Grubb, who was something of a stickler for the conventions, but also to the authorities whom Mr. Trumper talked about so glibly.

"Hey! You! Girl! Wake up! I didn't give you a lease of my bed."

She stirred. It seemed to take forever for her eyelids to lift and reveal the eyes, which were amazingly blue and at once made the rest of her white starved-cat face unimportant.

She frowned a little, as if she were having

difficulty in focussing her gaze. She didn't look alarmed, only puzzled, like someone in a dream. But when she tried to speak her voice was no more than a hoarse croak.

"I don't know where I am."

"You're in my bed," said Finch, with some indignation. "You should have gone by daylight. I left you money for lodgings."

The girl tried to sit up and failed. Her eyes widened. Now she did begin to look afraid.

"Why have you brought me here?"

"*I* didn't bring you here. You brought yourself. Uninvited. I don't want you to stay. I want you to go."

"In the dark?" she faltered.

"You should have gone by daylight," Finch said helplessly. "Lying there all day sleeping. And now you ask me why I brought you here. You were lying against my window this morning, like a bird brought down in a storm. I couldn't leave you in the street. Could I?" His voice rose reproachfully.

The girl drew the blanket up round her.

"My throat's awful sore."

19

"And no wonder! Sleeping in the street. Why did you do it? Where's your mother? Have you run away from home?"

"Home!" The word was a mere sigh. Her eyelids were dropping as if they were too heavy to hold up. Then suddenly they flew up to disclose again the incredibly blue eyes, dazed but burning like the sky in mid-summer. "You won't hurt me, will you?"

"Hurt you! Well, that's a question to ask! When I've left you here all day to sleep in my bed, and goodness knows what Mrs. Grubb is thinking. She'll have me out on my ear, most likely. I don't know. Honest, I don't. But I suppose you'd better have some supper. I can sleep on the floor for once. Mind you," he wagged a long ink-stained finger, "you'll have to go at the first sign of light."

"Mrs. Grubb?" she murmured, as if names and people frightened her more than the cold and the dark.

"I lodge with her. She lives upstairs. So we'll have to speak quietly. Could you fancy some soup?"

20

"Soup!" she echoed.

"It's only carrot," Finch apologised. "Nothing to whet your appetite. If I had known I was having company I'd have got in a joint and dumplings, and maybe a slice or two of partridge, and a bit of jugged hare, and jellies and trifles—Hey, how long have you been starving?"

He should have had more sense than to talk about food, clumsy oaf that he was. For the child's face had gone even whiter, if possible, and her eyes were closed. She muttered something about all that food making her feel sick, and then seemed to fall asleep, for Finch had to shake her awake when the soup was steaming in the enamel mug.

He found himself inordinately disappointed when she could swallow only a few spoonfuls, even though he patiently fed her himself. She would die if she went on like that, he thought worriedly, a tiny bit of porridge in the morning and now this bit of soup that wouldn't keep a cat alive. How was he to get rid of her tomorrow if she couldn't stand for weakness?

Bother the girl for collapsing at his window,

bother him for his soft-heartedness in taking her in instead of calling for Mrs. Grubb or setting off to inform the authorities.

Of course he could call Mrs. Grubb now, but she was probably already half into her nightly gin stupor, and would merely make ribald comments. Her loud voice ho-ho-ing knowingly at Finch would make that wild fright leap into the girl's face again. He couldn't bear his birds to be frightened, and already he was feeling the same about this scrap of humanity. "Well, I don't know," he said to himself. "I just don't know."

He stoked up the fire in the stove. It would be cold sleeping on the floor. Then he covered his birds, the linnets in one cage, the bullfinches in the other. Before he put out the lamp he took another look at his unwanted guest.

She seemed to be sound asleep, breathing in a quick shallow manner. Her hair was hopelessly snarled, but it looked as if it would be a pretty pale gold if it were washed. There was actually a bit of colour in her cheeks now, but it might be fever. He laid a finger on one to see. Then snatched it away, a sudden bewildering jolt in his body as if fever had struck him. He hadn't known a girl's skin was so soft and silky. He thought he knew so much. He could say how many miles it was to Van Dieman's Land, and New Zealand, what the climate was and the animal life, he could recite all the clauses of a lease of property in the City of London, or glibly quote yards of English laws on almost any subject at all, he had read avidly every book that came his way on the cultivation of land and the keeping of stock, and he knew the habits of most birds in the British Isles.

But he had never known the skin of a girl was so soft. . . .

It was a good thing, he reflected, that the floor was draughty and very hard and that he was promised a most uncomfortable night. That would make him adamant in the morning about getting rid of his uninvited guest.

In the very early morning she began to toss and mutter. Finch struck a match and saw, by the heavy silver watch that had been his father's, that it was only five o'clock. Then he had to light the candle by the bedside and hold it over the girl's face to see what made her so restless.

His heart sank when he saw the fever burning in her cheeks. It was as he had feared. She was sick. It would be out of the question to turn her out today, or tomorrow, or possibly even within a week.

"Hey!" he cried roughly, turning down the rumpled blanket. "What's wrong with you?"

Her blue gaze didn't recognise him. She cringed away and muttered hoarsely, "Don't! Don't! Don't, Mrs. Prichard!"

There was such distress in her voice that Finch couldn't help saying, "Who's this Mrs. Prichard? Who's been hurting a little bit of a thing like you?"

She stared at him as if she saw him, yet he knew she didn't, for the terror stayed in her eyes, and there was nothing in his homely face to terrify anybody.

"You've been having a bad dream," he said soothingly. "What's your name, love?"

Her eyes held a moment of stillness.

"Gilly," she said clearly. And then began to move restlessly again. "Don't let them get me! Please don't let them get me!"

At last he had to hold her in his arms to quieten her. She fell asleep with her tangled head against his shoulder. He could feel the heat of her body burning into him. He didn't know what to do. It was dawn and his birds were beginning to cheep. He couldn't be late at the office today. Mr. Trumper had meant those threats. There was only one thing to do and that was to call Mrs. Grubb.

As he feared, Mrs. Grubb was dismally sober. She stood at the door of her bedroom, her nightcap tilted askew over her irony-grey ringlets, her stout form wrapped in a voluminous red flannel dressing gown.

"Have I heard you right, Mr. Stevenson? A female in your room!"

Finch began to explain, but before he could finish Mrs. Grubb had brushed him aside, nearly setting alight to his eyebrows with her tilted candle, and swept off down the stairs.

She surveyed the girl in Finch's narrow bed for several incredulous moments. Then she said, "The fever hospital for her, Mr. Stevenson. I'll be surprised if she lasts the day."

"Oh, no, Mrs. Grubb!" Finch cried involuntarily, and earned himself a sharp suspicious stare from Mrs. Grubb's protuberant eyes.

"Eh, what's she to you? Are you telling me the truth?"

"You know I'm not the sort to have women down here," Finch replied with dignity.

"So far, I agree, you haven't been. So far you've lived an unnatural life with all this daft business about keeping birds in cages. But you're a healthy young man, I take it—"

Finch was blushing scarlet.

"Mrs. Grubb, you know my plans to save enough money to take my birds to New Zealand. That doesn't allow for an interest in the other sex. But I couldn't leave her to die in the street, could I?"

"No, I grant you, you couldn't," Mrs. Grubb agreed judicially. "Though there's many would doubt your motives. But why, if she's nothing

26

to you, do you object to taking her to the fever hospital?"

She was nothing to him. If he hadn't touched her skin, if he hadn't held her in his arms—

"She'll die there," he said rapidly. "You might as well put her back in the gutter. You know that's the truth. Look!" He snatched up the half crown he had left on the table. "This is yours if you'll look after her today while I'm at work. And tomorrow maybe. After that she'll be well and can go her own way."

Mrs. Grubb's eyes narrowed. "If she will. She may recognize a likely young man when she sees one." But her expression had become greedy at the sight of the money. "You'll be finding yourself with another passenger to take on your ship journey if you're not careful."

Finch threw back his head and gave his youthful shout of laughter.

"Her! You're daft yourself."

"Maybe." Mrs. Grubb bent over the sick girl. "She's nought but a child, at that. I'll need to make poultices for her chest. And she'll be

27

needing medicines and fresh milk. This half crown won't be enough."

"I'll give you another shilling," said Finch recklessly.

"Well, well," said Mrs. Grubb softly. "Well, well, well."

Rap went the ruler on his knuckles.

"Dreaming again, Mr. Stevenson," came Mr. Trumper's dry voice. "Did I omit to tell you that Mrs. Fairweather will be here at three to attest her will?"

"It will be ready, Mr. Trumper."

"It had better be, Mr. Stevenson. *And* a fair copy. And I want the Barclay settlement on my desk before you leave tonight. So you really can't afford to dream, can you, Mr. Stevenson?"

No, he couldn't afford to dream. A pair of terrified blue eyes couldn't be allowed to come between the parchment and the pen in his hand, and his wages at the end of the week, and the

29

trunk in which he had already packed his clothing, his mother's wedding ring, and a few treasured books.

Yet he couldn't get home quickly enough that night.

Mrs. Grubb swayed in the doorway. Her expression was no longer forbidding. The gin had already softened and sentimentalised her outlook toward Finch, her unwanted patient, and indeed the whole of humanity. She winked, her closed eye disappearing into the purple folds of her cheek.

"My word, young man, did you take a cab or did you run every step of the way. Impatient, eh? Anxious to see your little friend?"

"How is she, Mrs. Grubb? Is she better? Is she going to live?"

"She'll do, she'll do. And whoever talked of her dying, indeed."

"But remember," she called raucously after Finch's disappearing form, "I keep a respectable house. I'll have the conventions observed. That little fly-by-night goes when she can stand, or else—" her voice rose to a scream as she realised that she was losing her audience, "or else you'll make her an honest woman!"

The room was softly lit by the lamp on the table. It looked cosy, with the bit of curtain drawn across the window and the red embers in the stove. The birds were settling themselves to rest with little flutters and sleepy cheeps, and the girl in the bed was almost asleep, too.

But she started awake with her quick alarm when Finch bent over her.

"It's only me," he said. "I'm not going to hurt you. I told you that yesterday. Are you better?"

She nodded, her eyes enormous in her small face. She'd brushed her hair, or Mrs. Grubb had, and there seemed to be a great deal of it spread about the pillow. It would have looked wanton if it had sprung from any head but that little starved childish one.

"Did you eat something today?"

She became excited. "Mrs. Grubb gave me an egg. A whole egg!"

"You like eggs?"

"If as ever I get one."

Finch nodded understandingly, conscious of his own stomach hollow with hunger.

"It's made me strong. I'll be able to go to-morrow."

The blue eyes were very earnest. Finch contemplated them, and said, "Where'll you go? To that Mrs. Prichard?"

She shrank into the pillow. "How do you know about her?"

"You gabbled about her in the night. Is she someone who ill-treated you?"

"She was going to put me in jail. She wouldn't believe those men had stolen the ribbons from me. She said I made that up, even though my dress was torn and I was all muddied."

Finch sat on the edge of the narrow bed and bent his legal mind on this problem.

"You'll have to start at the beginning if I'm to know all the facts and make a judgment. Did you work for this Mrs. Prichard?"

"She's a milliner. I was apprenticed to her. We slept in the attic."

"Who?"

"Me and the other girls. She gave us gruel and turnip soup and bread, mostly. She was very strict. But it was all right until I lost the ribbons. I can sew well and she trusted me. But then she sent me to buy two rolls of French ribbon and on the way back two men set on me. They knocked me down in the mud and stole the parcel and my dress was ruined. I showed it to Mrs. Prichard, how it was spoiled, but she—" The girl started up on the pillow, her eyes blazing with indignation, "she said I was telling lies. I had kept the money and never bought the ribbon. She said I was to go, and slapped my face and—well, I had nowhere to go and no money." After a long pause when she seemed to be looking inwardly at what had happened since, she added, "She never paid us wages. She kept us, that was all."

"On turnip soup!" said Finch. "What did you do then?"

"I got a job as barmaid in the King's Tavern until—until the men—"

"And next?" said Finch roughly.

"There wasn't anything more. I seemed to be

always running away from someone—or hiding in a shed—or something." Her face brightened. "Once I found a whole loaf of bread dropped off a baker's tray. It rolled away. I had to be quick. I was ever so careful with it. It lasted four days."

Finch clenched his fists.

"How old are you, Gilly?"

"I don't know. Seventeen, I think. Or maybe eighteen."

He had a shock of surprise. She was a woman.

"Why don't you know? Don't you have any family? Any mother or father?"

"I was in a Home. That's where I learnt to sew. Mrs. Prichard liked girls from the Home because she didn't have to pay them wages."

"So you've got no family."

Her face went stubborn.

"I can manage. Mrs. Grubb has given me a gown and a shawl. I'll be strong enough to go tomorrow."

Finch looked at the small triangular face in its mass of luxuriating hair and thought the men would chase her for that hair. She should do it up under a bonnet, hide it. He wanted to tell her to do that. Anger was knotting inside him. She wasn't a child after all, in spite of her child's body. Didn't she know the streets were evil, corrupt, pitiless? Hadn't she learned not to flaunt a temptation? She should cut off her hair and keep her eyes downcast. Then she'd be nothing but a pale starved creature whom no one would look at.

"It's a rotten old world," he cried, banging his fist on the table, nearly upsetting the lamp. "That's why I'm leaving it."

"Leaving it!"

"In a maner of speaking. I'm emigrating. Me and my birds."

"To another country?"

"To New Zealand. I've saved nearly enough for my passage. I reckon to go in the spring."

"That's soon."

"Yes. I can't wait to see old Trumper's face."

"Old Trumper?"

"I work for him. I think he's a bit like your Mrs. Prichard. An old devil. Well, then. This won't get us a night's sleep. You have to be strong by morning and I have to be at work on the stroke of eight." He got up. "I'll just do my birds and have a bite of supper. Did you look at my birds?"

But the girl didn't answer. She had turned her face into the pillow and seemed to have fallen asleep. Just as quickly as that. Like a child. Safe and warm and fed. Finch nodded with a feeling of satisfaction, his anger dissolved. It was nice to think she was safe for a little while.

But he himself, in spite of his early rising and long day's work, felt restless and far from sleep. He cleaned out his birds' cages, working quickly so as not to disturb his sleeping companion. All his birds were looking healthy. Last week he had lost two blackbirds. They were hard to cage. But the linnets were lively and well-feathered, and the finches as cheeky as you please. He had hopes of getting another pair of blackbirds, but even if they survived here, he was doubtful if they would stand the long sea journey. There was the problem of taking the right sort of food for them, and the temperatures. Nell, his sister, wrote that it got awfully hot in the tropics, especially if the ship were becalmed. But he'd like to try again with the blackbirds.

Nell had written, "It's not easy here, it's no use my saying it is. I have to cook in the open, and the hut leaks in heavy rain, and if the baby is sick it's awful worrying. It's ten miles to the nearest neighbour where we live. But, oh, Finch, the trees and the birds and the sun! It's so free and sweet-smelling. Josh is going to plant two acres in potatoes next year, and we're getting another cow. Josh has never been so happy. And me, except I confess I get a bit homesick now and then. It's funny, the thing I miss most is the English birds. I keep thinking if only I could hear a blackbird singing, or a lark, I'd be perfectly happy. Josh says this is just a fancy of women in my condition. Oh, Finch, if only you were here to see little Josh, and the new baby, when it comes. . . ."

Finch finished cleaning the bird cages and covered them for the night. He looked towards the sleeping girl, suddenly resenting her slumber. He was used to being alone and used to keeping silent about his tremendous plans. But tonight the urge was on him to talk. He'd like to have seen Gilly's eyes grow big and awed as he talked about ships and new horizons. He'd tell her that he would take her down to the docks one day and show her the tall-masted ships preparing for their long voyages. When she had found some employment and was decently dressed and respectable he'd like to take her out walking on a Sunday.

She might like to come and wave him good-bye when he sailed. It would be nice to have someone to wave to.

Finch yawned, suddenly and hugely. Heigh ho for dreams. He would be better occupied in getting some sleep. He must be up, as usual, before dawn.

He was awakened some time later by a soft stirring in the room. He thought one of his birds must have escaped, but when he sat up and lit the candle he saw that it was the girl. She had her back to him and was struggling into some immense garment. As the light flickered she turned a startled face and said breathlessly, "I meant to be gone before you woke."

Finch sat up sharply. "Without breakfast? Without a thank you? That's manners for you."

"Oh, I didn't mean to be rude. I only thought you wouldn't think you had to feel responsible for me if I just went."

Her hair was tumbling round her face. When she finally got herself into the garment, a gown of Mrs. Grubb's that was much too big for her across the chest, she pushed her hair up, trying to knot it neatly in exactly the way Finch had thought it should be done. But without pins it fell down again, and suddenly the girl swayed, clutching a chair for support.

Finch leaped to his feet, thankful he had slept in his underclothes for warmth. He was decent, which was more than you could say for her, with that bodice falling off her narrow shoulders.

"You see!" he said severely, "you go out like that, weak and empty, and you'll be lying in the street again. Sit down. I'll fix some porridge.

39

And you'll have to make that gown fit better. And get some pins for your hair. You'll have to wait till Mrs. Grubb is up and that isn't till mid-morning. Waking her early would be more than your life's worth. She's in a rare temper first thing. Anyway, if you ask me, you can hardly stand. Hey, what's going on now?"

For she had begun to sob. Laying her head on the table, she sobbed and sobbed.

Finch was acutely disturbed. He couldn't stand the sight of those little shaking shoulders in the too large gown. She was a child dressed up and come to grief.

"Have I hurt you?" he demanded. "Have I been cruel and hard-hearted?"

Amid sobs and sniffs the tousled head gave a violent shake.

"Have I driven you out into the cold? Have I starved you? Didn't I leave you a half crown? Anyway, why should I support you, a complete stranger?" He was working himself into a fine anger. "What's it to me where you go or what you do?"

"N-nothing."

But it was. Looking down at her, he knew it was. He felt the same angry tenderness that he did for a bird damaged in a net. He wanted to take it home and nurse it back to life. He wanted to shake his fist and scream at all the people who inflicted cruelties on harmless creatures. That Mrs. Prichard, the old bitch. And all the nameless men who had persecuted a child, driving her into hiding and starvation.

Suddenly he knew that giving her half a crown and knowing she was warmly dressed was not enough. He would have to do more, find her a position and decent lodgings. It was no use to scream at the world's wrongs if he did nothing to right them. Besides, he hadn't shown her his birds properly. And his sea chest packed for travelling. It would be nice, he realised, if she were here when he came home tonight. They could talk. In such a short time he had almost got used to her being here.

He put his hand on her shoulder.

"Cheer up. I didn't mean to speak like that. I was only upset that you cried. You don't have to go today. You're not strong enough. You want feeding up. Can you cook?"

She lifted her tear-stained face warily.

"A little. Only plain cooking."

"Well, we won't be wanting anything fancy. But I tell you what, I'll leave you some money and you go to market and buy something for our supper tonight. Something tasty. How'd that be?"

"But—"

"Tomorrow you'll be stronger. If old Trumper's in a good mood—though, goodness knows, he never is—I'll ask him if he knows of a position for a good girl. And since I'm going to be late, wasting time talking to you, I'll have to leave you to uncover my birds and give them fresh water and seeds. Be careful how you open the cage doors. The finches are tame, but the linnets are nervous. If the sun shines they might sing to you."

Her face was quiet now, her eyes as large and solemn as a baby's.

"I don't even know your name."

"It's Edmund Stevenson, but everyone calls me Finch because of my birds."

"It's a grand name," she said. "Edmund Stevenson. I like Finch better."

A broad grin of pleasure spread over Finch's plain face.

"Do you?"

"It suits you," she said seriously. "I haven't got a last name. We were just all called Brown in the Home. Mary Brown, Susie Brown, Emma Brown, Gilly Brown. I don't know who called me Gilly. I suppose my mother did. I can't remember her."

"We're a pair, Gilly. My mother and father are both dead. My father was a country parson, but he died a long time since. I've only got my sister Nell in New Zealand. That's why I'm going there. But Lordy," he jumped up, "this won't get me to the office on time. You mix the porridge while I light the fire."

43

Mr. Trumper looked down his long parchment-coloured nose.

"And why so cheerful today, Mr. Stevenson? Have you had an unexpected windfall? Has someone left you a fortune? Or have you by any chance fallen in love?"

Beneath Mr. Trumper's sardonic scrutiny Finch found himself blushing furiously.

"I'm not especially cheerful, Mr. Trumper."

"Then stop that infuriating whistling, if you please. It gets on my nerves."

"I'm sorry, I didn't know I was whistling. It was unconscious."

"I hope your work isn't unconscious, too,"

Mr. Trumper snapped. "Get on with that Deed of Covenant as quickly as possible. Bless me, you're only at clause six. That won't do at all. Do your dreaming about your lady love out of office hours."

"I haven't got a lady love, Mr. Trumper."

He got a shrewd sour look from over Mr. Trumper's spectacles.

"I admit it would surprise me, Mr. Stevenson. I can't imagine what a young lady would see in you, to be sure."

Finch had no illusions himself about his attractions for the opposite sex. What would they see in him, with his plain face, his overgrown body, his shyness and awkwardness?

Yet Gilly did seem pleased to have him home that night. She had the lamp lit and the table laid and there was a savoury smell coming from the saucepan on the stove. The birds' cages were covered and the floor had been swept and polished. She herself looked a great deal better. There were smudges of pink in her cheeks and her hair was brushed and neatly braided. She had done something to Mrs. Grubb's gown, too, so that it didn't slip off her shoulders. She was still as slender as a willow branch, but she looked older. Grown-up, in fact. And demure, although her eyes danced with innocent pleasure at Finch's obvious delight. She began fussing over him, telling him to take off his coat and his muddied boots and sit himself by the fire, almost as if she were his wife.

Wife, thought Finch, struck with a peculiar pain in his heart. For it was the first time he had thought objectively about the day when he would take a wife. And what it would be like to be married.

That would come when he was settled in New Zealand. He would find a nice healthy hard-working girl and together they would conquer the wilderness and live in companionship and content.

"The butcher gave me bones for the stew," Gilly was saying. "He saw I was looking feeble so I made myself much more feeble. I nearly

46

swooned in front of him. He said to go home and make my husband look after me better." She laughed in a little gurgle. It was the first time he had heard her laugh. "My husband, if you please! Then I got the carrots and potatoes for only a penny."

"You're a bit of a witch, aren't you," Finch said tolerantly.

"And I cleaned the birds' cages," she went on. "And one linnet sat on my finger. Just for a second. And then the finches sang as if they were ever so pleased for clean cages. I was thinking that if you want to take birds to New Zealand you should have some sparrows. And robins. Surely they'd want robins."

"Some you can keep in cages and some you can't," Finch explained. "My blackbirds died. Robins would die, I'm afraid. But I've been meaning to try sparrows. I've a lad in Notting Hill who nets them in the lanes."

"We could get some sparrows," Gilly said eagerly, then bit her lip and flushed. "I didn't mean we—I'll be gone—but you could. And

47

now if you please will you sit down and have your supper."

The slip of her tongue had taken away her gaiety. She kept her head bent and ate her supper in silence. When they had both finished she took away the empty plates, then sat down again and said very soberly:

"I'm sorry I said that about them being our sparrows. It was because I was feeling so much better and it had been a lovely day. I'd felt so good, shopping and cooking for someone as—"

"Someone as what?" Finch prodded.

"As would be pleased for it."

"Well, I am pleased for it, so cheer up. Would you like to see my things? I mean the things I'm taking to New Zealand."

"I'll go tomorrow," she said.

"We'll see about that."

"I'll have to go," she said loudly, as if she suddenly thought him stupid. "I can't stay here. It isn't decent."

"Who says so?"

"Mrs. Grubb. She says now I'm not sick

any more—" Her voice faltered, and it was Finch's turn to be angry.

"You still look about as strong as a starved kitten. Who's Mrs. Grubb to say what's decent? Would it be decent to turn you out into the street without a job or a roof over your head?"

Gilly's head was bent.

"You were going to at first."

"I didn't know you then. Besides, I left you some money. But now it's different. You're my friend. You'll be staying here until I've found a job for you and know you're all right." He banged his fist on the table to emphasize this, and then sat back, surprised and baffled that he had allowed himself to get so carried away.

Anyway, she was his friend. It was true. She had cooked his meal and eaten with him. She had a look of charming dignity sitting opposite him. He would miss her when she had gone. He knew that already.

To take the wistful look off her face he pulled the brassbound chest from under his bed.

"I'll make a wager," he said, "that you don't even know where the colony of New Zealand is."

"It's a long ways," she volunteered.

"It's under the other side of the sky. It's got different stars. It's morning there when it's night here. Isn't that queer? I've got a map with it on it. I'll show you."

He extracted the much-creased much-loved map from his trunk and spreading it out on the table traced the route across the oceans to the tiny specks of red in the far corner.

"We go round the Cape of Good Hope. There are terrible storms there. And into the Indian Ocean where as like as not we'll be becalmed. There'll be flying fish and whales spouting. My sister Nell said they saw a sea monster rearing out of the deep."

Gilly's face was full of awe.

"Does it cost an awful lot to get there?

"It does. It's taken me long enough to save. But now I've got my passage booked on the *Flying Scud*. She sails at the end of March."

"When's that?"

"Don't you know the time of year, to be sure? It's just past the end of January. I go in two months. I'll soon have to break the news to old Trumper. That will be a rare pleasure, I can tell you. Look now, I'm taking my favourite books and a chess set. And Nell begged me to bring her some bonnet trimmings. Here's my father's Bible. It has all our names in it. See. Edmund Stevenson, born September 1836, Eleanor Stevenson born April 1839."

"And James Andrew Stevenson, born May 1840," Gilly read.

"Yes, that was Jamie. He died. He and my mother in the same week. My father wasn't ever the same again. But Nell's got a little lad now, and I'm going to have strong sons." Finch inflated his chest and Gilly said in an almost inaudible voice, "I expect you will. You're strong yourself. And with the sunshine and the good food in New Zealand—"

"You could do with a bit of that," Finch said heartily. "It's a pity you can't come. Would you be scared?"

"Scared?" Her blue eyes looked up at him. "What of?"

"That long sea voyage. They say folks get sick and sometimes go mad."

"Oh, that," she said with a slight scornful lift of her shoulders. "I wouldn't be scared of that."

But in the night he heard his narrow ricketty bed shaking and he thought she was crying again.

He sat up, realising how chilly and stiff he was from lying on the floor.

"What's the matter?"

"I'm cold."

Finch was at a loss.

"I haven't got another blanket. Put your gown over you."

"I have. It's still—" he knew that in the dark she was hugging her arms round herself, "—awful cold."

Finch became more conscious of icy draughts along the floor. He got up and pulled the curtains aside to look out of the window.

"No wonder! It's snowing! You'd better have my blanket."

"And then you'll freeze!"

"No, I won't. I'll light the fire." He was thinking of his small supply of fuel, meant to last another week. "Or else—"

"Else what?"

"Else I'll lie beside you and we'll keep each other warm."

He heard her startled movement. There was a little silence. Then she said, "I don't take up very much room," and he could hear her moving over in the bed.

He lay on the top, pulling his blanket over him. There was enough room so long as they lay close. Indeed, it was surprisingly comfortable. After a while, Gilly stirred and murmured sleepily, "Now it's warm."

Finch awoke in the dark dawn to find her hair across his face. And it was all right for it to be strewn lavishly like that for him. A woman's hair, he thought, was a private thing, meant to be displayed in its full glory only to her husband.

53

Gilly's husband. . . . Well, that was a daft thought with which to be waking.

The snow lay thick on the ground. The air was iron grey, the cold petrifying.

"You aren't going anywhere today," Finch said definitely. "You'll stay here and keep a fire burning." (He would have to be reckless with his fuel in this inclement weather.) When he saw the doubt in her face he said, "My birds will die of cold without a fire, and someone will have to tend it."

"What will Mrs. Grubb say?"

"Mrs. Grubb can mind her own business for once. If she comes over righteous you can ask her what she thinks I am, a child seducer?"

Gilly giggled, with her sudden young delight.

Then she said with intense seriousness, "I think you're the kindest man I ever met."

"Pshaw!" Finch was embarrassed and hugely pleased. "Ask old Trumper about that."

But he thought the day would never end so that he could get home again to the firelight and the sleepy twittering of his birds, and her welcoming face.

54

It couldn't go on, of course. But while the snow lasted, you wouldn't turn a dog outdoors.

Mrs. Grubb didn't see it that way. After the second night she came clattering down the narrow stairs and thumped on the door.

"You lovebirds!" she called raucously. "It won't do. The whole street's talking."

Finch threw open the door and stood towering over the irate Mrs. Grubb who wore her sour morning face.

"The street can mind its business and I'll mind mine. What I do is my own affair."

"It's mine, too, Mr. Stevenson. This is my house. And I've kept it respectable since Grubb passed on. There's Miss Armitage upstairs and you, a nice quiet young gentleman, so I thought, in the basement. I didn't bargain for any fly-by-nights."

Finch reached for Gilly's hand and drew it into his own.

"This is no fly-by-night," he said in a low fierce voice. "And you know it. If you want her to freeze to death in the streets to save your respectability, then you're a vicious old creature with a stone for a heart. If you do turn her out then I go, too, and you can have your precious respectable room."

"And where would you go, my fine gallant?" Mrs. Grubb screamed.

Her anger touched off Finch's own.

"To New Zealand. We'd emigrate. We'd leave this black freezing place where everyone's heart has shrivelled up with meanness. We'd sail on the first ship that would take us—" He felt Gilly's hand tighten in his own and suddenly, in a great flash, he knew he wasn't just making idle threats to an intimidating landlady. He was speaking the truth. It was what he had wanted to do, without knowing it. To have Gilly beside him on the lifting deck of the ship, to see her growing strong and rosy-cheeked in the warm winds.

Really, he had known ever since the night he had lain beside her that he couldn't let her go. Or earlier than that. When he had first seen the summer blue of her eyes.

"We'll be married first, of course," he said pedantically.

Then Gilly did gasp, drawing her hand away, and at the same time Mrs. Grubb's face changed subtly to her purple-flushed knowing winking evening one.

"Ho, ho, Mr. Stevenson! So it's come to that. I thought it would. I thought you was too decent not to propose marriage. Well, this puts another light on the matter. I always did have a soft heart for young love. I'll give the bride a gown to be married in. And a bonnet and shoes, and—dear me, child, I expect you haven't even a decent petticoat. Leave it all to me. Leave it all to Mrs. Grubb. My, what a romance! How I do envy a young romance."

The moment she had gone, clucking in a satisfied manner, Gilly turned on Finch, her eyes blazing, her cheeks scarlet.

"You stupid, stupid creature! How can you do anything so crazy?"

"It came over me," Finch confessed. "I know I should have spoken to you privately

first. But it just came over me. And it isn't
crazy!"

"But it is! You've ruined all your plans. How
can you sail on the *Flying Scud* now? You said
you'd saved for a long time to get your ticket.
You didn't say you were taking a wife. You
can't afford to take a wife!" She stood back,
breathing quickly. "What about your sister?
What about your birds?"

"Nell will have to wait. So will my birds. So
will you. You see, all I have to do is to postpone my passage until I can save enough to buy
another one for you. We could do it in a year
or so, if you help. You can get jobs here and
there. And I'm due soon for a rise in my wages.
It'll be more fun doing it together, you must
admit that. Look here, let's sit down and write
to Nell and tell her. Let's say I'm taking a wife,
so there'll be two of us coming."

Her anger had died.

"I didn't expect to be married out of pity."

"Pity!" said Finch slowly, looking at her, so
small, so drab in Mrs. Grubb's old gown, a little London sparrow, except for those great

58

blue eyes. His tongue tripped a bit with shyness and his queer growing excitement.

"I'd say it was more out of love," he said.

To that, she had nothing to say at all.

True to her word, Mrs. Grubb made a silk gown for Gilly with her own hands. She was a good seamstress. To be sure, she had chosen grey silk as a good practical colour, but she had put a ruching of Nottingham lace round the high neck, and made a grey bonnet with a wreath of artificial violets round the brim. Finch came home with a posy of early snowdrops. They were very frail and Gilly clutched them so tightly that they had wilted before the minister, in Mrs. Grubb's parlour, had even got to the "With this ring I thee wed." When he did say that Finch slipped his mother's wedding ring, which he had been going to take to New

Zealand for another bride, on to Gilly's finger, and then found it was so big she could scarcely keep it on.

But she fiercely refused to have it altered. She would wear it on her middle finger, she said, and be just as securely married.

"Bless the child!" said Mrs. Grubb, mopping tears, and offering cups of tea or glasses of porter all round.

Naturally the newly married couple could not do anything so extravagant as go on a honeymoon. Instead, as soon as they could escape from Mrs. Grubb's hospitality, they walked down the muddy streets, still flecked with snow, to the office of the shipping company in Cheapside. There, Finch introduced his bride and said that now they would require a ticket in the names of Mr. and Mrs. Stevenson. The one he held in his own name for a passage on the *Flying Scud*, he would like transferred to a suitable ship sailing in approximately a year's time.

"So you're taking your wife." The clerk was sympathetic. "A good idea, if I may say so. A man gets lonely in a new country. I've heard of many unfortunate cases. Loneliness, homesickness, even suicide. But with a wife to make you a home in the wilderness the picture is quite different."

"You see," said Finch to Gilly, out in the street again. "Wasn't I right to marry you?"

"It's an awful long time to wait."

"It's not that long. Let's go home and look at the map again. I'll show you where we'll begin to feel the hot monsoons, and where we'll get the smell of spice drifting from tropical shores. And where we make the acquaintance of Father Neptune. He's supposed to come up out of the deep with his long beard dripping with seaweed. Hey, what are you crying for?"

"I shouldn't have done it. I shouldn't have held you back. You've been caught. One day you'll blame me."

He had to take her shoulders and shake her.

"But I wanted to be held back. I wanted to be caught. Bless me, for all the worriting creatures—"

"There's a light like stars in your eyes when you talk about sailing. It mightn't still be there in a year."

"Why ever not?" he asked in amazement. "What's to put it out?"

He thought back to that conversation in the early hours of the morning, when he awoke to the still new and astonished delight of finding her in his arms, no blanket separating them now. He had found her body, so young and fragile, yet so much a woman's. With all of her silken skin free to the touch of his hands a kind of madness had seized him. His little Gilly, his wife, his beloved. . . . And she had thought she might put the stars out of his eyes!

In the morning she said, "Get out your father's Bible, Finch."

When he did so, she said, "Write me in it."

She leaned over his shoulder, watching as he did so, "Edmund Stevenson married Gilly Brown on the 2nd February 1860." When he had finished she gave a sigh. For the first time she looked happy.

In his usual pessimistic way Mr. Trumper deplored Finch's rashness in taking a wife.

"You're scarcely fit for the responsibility of writing out a Deed of Covenant, correctly, Mr. Stevenson. You have a head full of sawdust as far as I can ascertain. Always day-dreaming, always in a brown study. How does that go with keeping a wife?"

"My dearest Finch, I am so happy you have taken a wife," wrote Nell. "Josh and I and little Josh wish you every happiness. Naturally we are disappointed that you must postpone your journey here, but a year will soon pass. I still long to hear your birds in the trees out here, but I look forward even more to meeting your Gilly. I hope she is a good housewife. . . ."

She was. Finch came home with a light step every night to find the little room shining with cleanliness and his supper on the table. There was a geranium in a pot on the windowsill between the bird cages because birds liked to see growing things, Gilly said, and already she had made a rag mat to take the chill off the stone floor, and was at work on a patchwork quilt. She shopped economically and sensibly at the market, and when her housekeeping was done she worked six hours a day selling buttons and sewing thread in Mrs. Bunch's haberdashery shop on Fish Street. Mrs. Grubb had spoken to Mrs. Bunch and Mrs. Bunch had been taken by Gilly's neatness and civility.

At the end of each week they laid their wages on the table and carefully counted what could be set aside. The sovereigns in the tin hidden beneath the loose floorboard grew slowly but surely. It was summer and the birds loved the sun coming through the window. The linnets sang madly. The boy on the farm at Notting Hill brought in two more blackbirds and so far they had thrived. On Sundays Finch made Gilly put on her sunbonnet and come for long walks in the country lanes between Chelsea and Kensington. Sometimes they rode on an omnibus all the way to Hampstead Heath.

They never talked of love. Finch had never heard Gilly say she loved him. But she lay willingly in his arms. Sometimes she teased him gently about his big nose and plain face. She liked to hold his hand when they went out walking. They talked all the time about New Zealand. Or Finch talked and Gilly listened.

The summer slipped by and they had half of Gilly's fare saved. They began to talk of household things to take, linen and blankets. They didn't want to arrive like paupers. It would postpone their sailing another three or four months if they were to acquire these things, but now Finch insisted. He wasn't going to have his sister saying he hadn't provided for his bride.

66

"You see," said Gilly, "without me you wouldn't have needed these things. You'd just have taken your sea chest and your birds."

"What's another few months?" Finch demanded. "Is it so hard to wait? Aren't you happy?"

"I can't bear to hold you back. You would be there by now if it hadn't been for me."

"I asked, are you happy?"

"Oh, yes, yes," she said fervently, but looked about to cry. He couldn't make her out. Didn't she like living in Mrs. Grubb's basement room with him?

Mrs. Bunch, through having a haberdasher's shop, was able to get household linen cheap, through a warehouse. Gilly's spirits rose again. When Finch talked of strange birds called tuis and wekas, and acres of luxuriating tree farms, and mudholes that bubbled with steam rising out of them, and the Maori with his melodious songs, she hung on his words. London, Mrs. Grubb's house, old Trumper, the teeming streets, the freezing fogs and misery, disappeared from their minds. They were already embarked.

Until the night just before Christmas when Finch came home and found Gilly white-faced and quiet. He thought she must be ill.

"What's the matter? Are you sick?"

She shook her head very slowly. She wouldn't look at him as she said, "I'm going to have a baby."

After a moment of consternation he said too quickly, "But that's wonderful! Me a father! Lordy!"

He wasn't prepared for her flinging herself at him and beating his breast.

"Don't pretend! You're not pleased. You're as upset as I am. It's awful, awful!"

"Now listen, Gilly love—"

"Don't *pretend!* You know it means we can't go. We'll have to wait."

"Wait? I hadn't thought—"

"Then you must think. Because I can't have the baby born on a ship. It would die. Haven't you told me how many children die on that

68

voyage! And a new-born baby—even for you, I won't let it be born on the ship."

"No, a ship isn't the best place to have a baby," Finch agreed soberly. "You're right. We couldn't take that risk. We'll have to wait until the baby's born, and is well and strong. We can do that easy. It won't be so long."

"It will be about another year."

She was right. Nearly nine months for the baby to come, and then three for it to grow strong. . . . He couldn't be expected to take that in all at once.

Another year of old Trumper's tyranny. Another year of keeping his birds alive and of living themselves like moles underground. Then travelling with a small baby, the clothes, the extra luggage, the money. Old Trumper hadn't been so far out when he had talked of the responsibilities of marriage. It had been so simple before.

Before Gilly? Finch was overcome by his treachery. He tilted her woebegone face upwards for a kiss.

"What's another year now we've waited this

long? A baby! It might be a son! Are you making me a son, little Gillyflower?"

Her face seemed to tremble, the blue eyes drowned.

"Oh, I hope so, Finch. I say my prayers that it will be—to make up."

"And don't you talk that nonsense! What are you having to make up for?"

Mrs. Grubb was in her element now. She loved pregnancies even more than marriages. She knew of an excellent midwife. "Only the best, Mr. Stevenson," and made a sinister remark about "your wife being so narrow."

She also instructed Gilly in the preparation of the baby's trousseau, and what with the purchase of knitting wool, yards of flannel and winceyette, Finch found their precious savings having to be dipped into more and more. It didn't matter, he said fiercely, but Gilly's forlorn face showed she didn't believe him. The strange formless scrap of life inside her, which should have been so dearly loved, was like a white ant gnawing away at the foundations of their future.

Finch did extra work at the office, bending over his documents sometimes until nearly midnight. It was hardly worth it, for old Trumper, rubbing his hands evilly and commenting on the joys of marriage, paid him only a pittance over and above his weekly wage.

The winter went by at last, and the *Flying Scud* sailed again without Mr. Edmund Stevenson and four cages of song birds on board.

Gilly's face was far too small and sharpened for her swollen body, but with the discomfort of late pregnancy she developed a wistful gaiety that made Finch want to both laugh and cry. She insisted on having the Bible out of the trunk so that the birth could be written in it immediately.

"Fancy me having something to put in your Bible," she said. She seemed immensely proud of this, as though she would have made a lasting inscription on the world. Finch often had to take her hands and say, "Wake up! You're a hundred miles away."

Once she said, "Please don't hate me, Finch."

"Hate you! Are you crazy?"

"You could, without knowing."

And then one of the linnets died, and she was in floods of tears.

"It's been kept in a cage too long. It's all my fault."

"It's died of old age," said Finch stoutly. "I expect it was an old bird when I got it. It would have died in a hedge in the winter long ago if it had been free."

"Not if it had been in New Zealand," she insisted stubbornly.

Finch wisely put this persnickety behaviour down to her state of health. And indeed it was the true explanation, for her labour pains began that night.

He was scared to death. He galloped upstairs to rouse Mrs. Grubb who scolded him peevishly. But when the news penetrated her gin-stupefied brain she pulled herself together with surprising alacrity and sent him off for the midwife.

73

Then they all gathered in the little basement room which grew hotter and hotter as kettles boiled on the roaring stove. The midwife, after casting an experienced eye over her patient, gave it as her opinion that the birth was some hours off. "She's terribly narrow," she said in a disapproving voice, and the word again struck a chill in Finch's heart.

He sat by the bed and held Gilly's hand until, towards morning, it grew too hot and clenched and she writhed away from him. He wanted to beg her to let him bear her pain. "Put it all on me," he wanted to say. But the words stuck in his throat. He kept thinking of the way she had clutched the little posy of snowdrops on her wedding day until they had wilted. Now she seemed to be wilting in his hands.

The midwife, who had been knitting cosily by the fire, came back to look at her patient. She was kind now, and Finch could have hugged her for her kindness.

"Scream, dearie, if you want to. Scream your head off." She looked at Finch. "You'd better get out, young man. This is no place for you, though bless my soul if you shouldn't be made to watch every bit of the results of your work."

Mrs. Grubb said Finch could wait in her parlour. He was promised he would be called the moment there was any news. He bent over Gilly, reluctant to leave her, but she didn't seem to recognise him any longer. She was moaning now, and the little sounds wrenched from her throat seemed as if they were torn out of his own heart. He went blindly upstairs to wait.

Two interminable hours later Mrs. Grubb came bustling up in great alarm.

"You must go for the doctor. Mrs. Murphy can't manage without a doctor."

"What's wrong? What's wrong?" Finch shouted.

"She's too narrow. I said so all the time. Run for Doctor Higgins. He's at the end of Bread Street. You'll see his plate."

The sun was up, Finch realised in astonishment. He should be at the office. Old Trumper would be in a rare taking. The streets were busy, with barrow boys and crossing-sweepers, and cabs, and clerks hurrying off to shops and offices. He bumped into an old woman pushing a barrow full of junk, and nearly fell under the wheels of a dray.

He was out of breath and scarcely able to speak when he reached Doctor Higgins. And all the time he knew it was no use.

As the sun stood half-way down the sky on a wintry noon they told him he had a son and it was dead.

He blundered out into the street, the tears pouring down his cheeks. He didn't come back till dark and by that time Gilly was deep in an exhausted sleep. So he couldn't explain what had possessed him to run away. In any case he didn't entirely know.

When Mr. Trumper saw, the next day, that his imprecations were having no effect on this wild haggard young man, he stopped them and said sourly:

"Very well, Mr. Stevenson, in view of the tragic circumstances I'll say no more about your absence yesterday. I'm not a man without a heart. Mr. Sampson's instructions were to dismiss you immediately, but I'll venture to intercede for you. You'll remember that I expressed doubt as to whether you were ready for the responsibilities of marriage. Your lamentable display can hardly have been of help to your wife. Be a man, Mr. Stevenson, be a man!"

"Curse you!" whispered Finch under his breath.

What did Mr. Trumper think he cared for his dead son so long as Gilly was alive? And yet he hadn't been able to say this to her. She had looked so white and small, as frail as thistledown, when she had woken in the morning. He hadn't dared to touch her. And again the tender words had stuck in his throat. He was a great inarticulate clumsy oaf, not even able to tell his wife how he loved her.

But he would show her in other ways. He dipped recklessly into their savings and bought her a new gown. He paid the doctor and the midwife. He saw that now they wouldn't be able to pay for their passage to New Zealand until next Christmas, at the earliest. But it didn't matter. He showed Gilly it didn't matter by stopping talking about New Zealand altogether. He bought little delicacies, fresh country eggs, a wing of chicken, even a half pound of real butter, to make her grow strong.

But it was funny, now he had stopped mentioning ships and sailing and new colonies, there didn't seem much to talk about. And with the way he had been spending money, nothing was added to their depleted savings.

It didn't matter. There was plenty of time. On a warm spring evening Finch made Gilly come for a long walk away from the noisy odorous streets to the sweet-smelling lanes near Notting Hill. To his joy, a nightingale began to sing. He stopped to listen, his arm close round Gilly's waist.

"There! Isn't that beautiful! My linnets could sing like that if they were free."

She stared up into his face in the dusk. She seemed to be trying to look inside his skull. He had never seen her so intense.

"What is it, love? Haven't you ever heard a nightingale before?"

She suddenly buried her face against his breast. She didn't say anything at all. But he understood. The words were stuck in her throat as they had too often been in his.

He had always teased Gilly about her spelling. She hadn't been taught much spelling in the Home, she defended herself. Anyway, she wasn't clever.

But he found nothing to laugh about in the quaintness of the note left on the table. It was there when he came home from the office the following evening.

My deer Husband,

               I am leeving you. Dont try to find me or worry about me. Go on the next ship sailing. Take your birds befor they all die. Pleese. Pleese. I

no I had cort you for too long. You are
not a person to be cort.

> I will love you allways.
>
> Gilly.

He burst into Mrs. Grubb's parlour unceremoniously, like a madman.

"Where's my wife? Have you seen my wife?"

"Mr. Stevenson!" Mrs. Grubb started up, alarmed. "Calm yourself, pray. I don't know where your wife is. Has she gone to the market?"

"She's left me!" Finch cried in a strangled voice. "She's gone away."

He couldn't be calmed. He waved away a stiff noggin of gin and said he was going out to search for Gilly. "I'll find her. I'll bring her back in an hour."

"Why should she run away? Have you been cruel to her?"

"She thought she was holding me back from going to New Zealand. She thought it was her fault. She says to take my birds and go without her."

"If you made her see you wanted it that much," said Mrs. Grubb shrewdly, "then you'd better go."

"I never told her I loved her," Finch said despairingly. "Not properly. I've got to find her and tell her."

"There's several million people in London, Mr. Stevenson. It won't be easy."

"I'll find her," said Finch. "Does she think she can hide from me?"

But she could. All summer Finch looked for her, tramping the streets until midnight, arriving at work haggard and exhausted the next day, and, while he wrote documents in his meticulous script, planning where he would look on the coming night.

He searched Cheapside and Bow Bells, Stepney, Shoreditch, Bethnal Green. He even went up through the West End to Knightsbridge and Kensington thinking she might have obtained a position as maid in one of the big houses. He enquired in shops and public houses and lodging houses. Had anyone seen his wife, a small slight creature, nothing much to look at except for her large blue eyes.

He got sympathised with and laughed at and had doors slammed in his face. It was a lovely summer, hot and still. The blue sky mocked him. He walked down the Notting Hill lanes and listened to the birds and smelt the wild parsley and sweet briar. He kept thinking he saw Gilly in the distance, just too far off to catch. Once he grabbed the shoulder of a slim-waisted girl with heavy bright hair, and spun her round, only to be spat at as he saw her hard strange face. He began to dream about her every night, thinking she was lying beside him, and woke tortured to the empty place in the bed.

As autumn came he began to haunt the river, leaning over the embankment, mesmerised by the slow-flowing muddy water. The fogs came, and the foghorns sounded, and the barges, black, silent, bier-shaped, slipped down the stream.

But there were other boats, too, and, if he went as far as London docks, he found the big ships, their masts towering in the mist above him. He smelled the strange exciting smells, salt, oil, a hint of spice from the cargo of a Far East trader, over-ripe fruit, the sourness of the bilge. The seagulls wheeled and shrieked overhead and something began to stir again in Finch.

"You're nothing but a skeleton, Mr. Stevenson," Mrs. Grubb clucked. "It's time you stopped fretting and did what she wanted you to. Otherwise you'll go into a decline, and where's the sense of that?"

"You mean leave here? Emigrate?" Finch said hoarsely.

"Yes, get away," Mrs. Grubb said firmly. "She knows you've always been fretting to go. She knows you better than you do yourself, I'm thinking. Take your birds and start a new life. Not that I won't miss you. But I can't a-bear to see a healthy young man wasting away to a shadow."

He would do it. Mrs. Grubb was right. Gilly had set him free for this, so he must follow her wishes.

He found he could get a berth on the *Mary Jane* sailing in November. It was so soon that it didn't give him time to think any more. He sent off an excited letter to his sister telling her he might arrive before the letter. The money he had left after paying for his ticket he gave to Mrs. Grubb to keep in trust for Gilly if ever she should turn up. Then he told Mr. Trumper, and that gentleman baffled him completely by proving he had a heart after all.

"I don't mind telling you, Mr. Stevenson, I've grown used to you. I shall miss you. I think you're taking a great risk going so far. Into unknown dangers. But I daresay our Queen looks to you young people to populate her colonies. I wish you luck, Mr. Stevenson."

His birds were in fine fettle. He had thirteen healthy linnets, six finches, and a dozen lively sparrows cheeping and twittering busily all day. The master of the *Mary Jane* was perfectly willing for him to accommodate them in his cabin so long as they were not a nuisance to the rest of the passengers. There were sheep, a placid Jersey cow, and an assortment of poultry in the hold.

"A sailing ship nowadays is a travelling menagerie," Captain Bolt said cheerfully. "We make no guarantee to land every living creature alive. But we do our best. Be on board at noon tomorrow, sir. We sail on the afternoon tide."

He said his goodbyes. There were not many. He had been a solitary young man immersed in his dream until Gilly had come. Now he was solitary again.

He gave a boy with a barrow two-pence to wheel his sea chest to the docks. He carried the bird cages himself. He didn't want his birds too frightened or jostled about. They must be in good health at the end of the long journey.

The *Mary Jane* was full of the bustle of sailing. Her decks were crowded with emigrants waving last goodbyes to their families and friends on shore. There was much joking and badinage, and, too often, the sound of weeping.

There was no one to wave goodbye to him. Finch stood alone at the back of the crowd, his

86

travelling coat not warm enough to withstand the chill breath of the water and the dark mid-November day. There was mist wreathing the drab dock buildings, making them less ugly. The figures down on the wharf were wrapped in the vague softening stuff, too. He could see the faces of women, white and wraithlike, up-turned to the deck. The gulls wheeled in and out of the dimness, screeching. It was all melancholy, sad, an ending to part of his life.

If Gilly had been at his side it would have been a beginning. He would have hugged her and laughed to see the dreary dockside, the gateway to London slums, disappearing. He would have—

Finch's thought was never finished for suddenly, in the mist, he saw her. Standing alone, a little distance from the crowd, her shawl wrapped tightly round her slim shoulders, her bright hair free. She was staring at the ship, staring at him with such intensity that he could have sworn she saw him.

However, this couldn't be so, for when he rushed to the rail crying joyfully to her she

87

turned and he could no longer see her face. She was just a dark shape, withdrawn from the crowd, lonely. . . .

Without a thought for his birds, his books, his clothes, his Bible, all his worldly goods, Finch pushed through the crowd, thrusting people out of his way.

The gangway was about to be taken up.

"Wait!" he shouted. "Wait! I'm coming ashore!"

He blundered down the rough steps in three strides. Hands clutched at him, voices congratulated him, thinking he was not a traveller and had nearly been mistakenly carried out to sea. He heard the gangway rattling up behind him, but he didn't turn to see the *Mary Jane* move inch by inch into midstream. He was flying down the street through the deepening fog shouting, "Gilly! I'm coming! Wait!"

She couldn't have disappeared so quickly. He didn't believe it. But there was only a small stunted tree on the corner where he had seen her, its twisted branches hung with dilapidated autumn leaves. *How* could he have thought it was a woman? How could he have had such an hallucination? Had his love and longing conjured Gilly out of thin air, only to vanish again?

He refused to believe it. He searched the mean streets until after dark, when the *Mary Jane* would be putting out into the open sea.

Exhausted, numbed, in despair, he realised what had happened. He had lost his birds, uncared for and dying on the ship, all his possessions and his passage to New Zealand. But without Gilly all was lost anyway. Lost, lost, lost . . .

Mrs. Grubb exclaimed, "My boy! My poor dear!" and quite forgot her careful formality. "Whatever happened? Did you miss the ship?"

When, in short difficult sentences, Finch told her, she began to weep, her tears more than a little helped by the gin bottle at her elbow.

"My poor boy, you're the victim of a delusion. But what feelings you have! Dearie me, I believe you will expire of love."

In the morning she was more practical. She said that naturally Finch could have his old room, but he had better go off to his office at once and see if there was any chance of getting his job back.

"Because if you're going to remain an English citizen after all, you will have to earn your daily bread."

Finch did everything she told him. He heard her voice perfectly clearly, although the sound of the gulls crying and the slap of water against the *Mary Jane* was louder in his ears. And although he made his way to Fleet Street quite safely among the jostling traffic, he saw nothing but that wraith in the mist, that face beckoning him.

Mr. Trumper reacted much as Mrs. Grubb had done. He said that although Finch's position had been filled, the new clerk was most unprepossessing, idle, careless, and with deplorably bad teeth. It was probable that Mr. Stevenson could be accommodated again. He would speak personally to Mr. Sampson.

Though Mr. Stevenson had better remember the virtues of punctuality, neatness, politeness, humility. The ruler cracked warningly on the desk, making the new young man with the bad teeth nearly fall off his stool with fright.

So life went on as it had done, except that

now he had no heart to keep more birds, and it seemed as if the winter would never end. Not that that mattered. It was better for his life to be in ruins in the bitter weather than when the sky was a summer blue.

Somehow, time did go by. Late in the spring a letter arrived from Nell.

He didn't want to open it. It would be full of reproaches. What had happened to him? Was he ever coming?

When he tore open the flap a newspaper cutting fell out. He picked it up listlessly and began to read.

Residents in the rapidly growing town of Wellington are accustomed to the cries of native birds, the delicate chime of the bellbird, the tui's liquid note, and the busy chatter of flirting fantails. But this morning they were treated to a rare surprise. Mr. Samuel Brown of Victoria Avenue reported hearing English linnets singing from the matapo tree in his garden. Unable to believe his ears he fetched his wife and

92

she bore witness to the fact that two linnets appear to have taken up residence in his garden.

"It was like a voice from home," Mrs. Brown declared in happy tears.

The mystery was later solved by the master of the newly-arrived *Mary Jane* admitting that he had done all he could to keep alive several cages of birds left aboard his ship by a passenger who at the last moment, overcome by separation from his loved ones, did not sail. All but four linnets had died, and these he had released as soon as he put into harbour.

We all pray that these welcome newcomers will thrive and be the forerunner of the arrival of more English birds, to stir fond memories of our beloved homeland.

Finch sat for a long time with the newspaper cutting in his hand. He re-read it a dozen times, criticising its florid style, while all the time the warm certainty grew within him.

If such a thing could happen, if his deserted

birds could travel thirteen thousand miles over trackless oceans and survive to sing in a new country, then he could find Gilly again. She was here, somewhere. He would find her, perhaps not this week or the next, but sometime. Nothing, he knew now, was impossible. Nothing.

He hummed a little as he put on his boots, lacing them methodically, not rushing. He wouldn't rush about wildly any more. He would search quietly, persistently, undefeatedly.

He noticed, as he went up the steps into the street, that it was mid-summer. It was June, arriving on him unawares, and the street, in the pale yellow evening light, looked curiously washed and softened and beautiful.

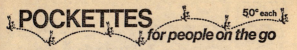